CAROLINA PRAYER

A North Carolina meditation of thankfulness

BY BRIAN FAULKNER

MANN MEDIA, INC.

publisher of *Our State* magazine

Copyright © 2003; Brian Faulkner
Photography Copyright © 2003; Kevin Adams and Gene Stafford
Published by Mann Media, Inc.
Post Office Box 4552, Greensboro, North Carolina 27404
Printed in China by C&C Offest Printing Co., Ltd.

Front and Back Cover photography by Kevin Adams
Author *Brian Faulkner*
Editor *Vicky Jarrett*
Senior Editor *Elizabeth Hudson*
Marketing Director *Amy Wood*
Production Manager *Cheryl Bissett*
Art Director *Larry Williams*
Distribution Manager *Erica Derr*

Library of Congress Cataloging-in-Publication Data

Faulkner, Brian, 1943-
  A Carolina prayer : a North Carolina meditation of thankfulness / by
Brian Faulkner.
      p. cm.
  ISBN 0-9723396-2-0 (hardcover : alk. paper)
  1. North Carolina—Pictorial works. 2. Prayers. 3. Meditations. I.
Title.
  F255.F38 2003
  975.6—dc21

                        2003011178

A Carolina Prayer *is dedicated to all those who love North Carolina —*
in all our quiet places, may you find serenity and peace.

Great God in Heaven,
we thank you for our state,
this Carolina,
this Eden of the East.

We thank you for her foggy,
blue-tinged mountains,
for every fold and valley,
for mountain folk and folkways.

*We thank you for
the very air we breathe,
the music we make,
and the songs we sing.*

*We thank you for
every hillside flower.
We thank you for the snow.*

*We thank you for
the Piedmont, Lord,
for its hustle and promise.*

We thank you for our people, too,
— native and newcomer alike —
weaver, knitter, driver, teacher, performer, preacher,
artist, and storekeeper; for doctors, nurses, bankers,
and business people; for students, farmers, firefighters,
and those who keep the peace;
for pets — and the mail.

We thank you, as well,
for gentle spring
   and the glory of autumn.

We thank you
for the Sandhills,
for its loblollies,
soldiers, and small towns;
for its products
from the land,
proud people,
and rare beauty.

We thank you for lakes and rivers,
for rushing stream, lazy creek, and sultry swamp —
for every pond and puddle.
We thank you for the wind and the rain.

We thank you for the Coastal Plain,
    for its centers of learning and research ...
for those who govern and build and sell;
    for those who work with their hands;

for mother, daughter, father, son;
    for husbands and wives, grandmas
and grandpas, cousins — and for babies.

*We thank you for roads
and parks, cars and trucks;
for planes and trains, buses and boats
and tractors — and for bicycles.*

We thank you for the sun.
And we thank you for shore and sea,
which beckons to us all —
from daybreak's first blush
to the last tints of gold
that paint the coast in rich,
satisfying colors at the end
of a long summer's day.

We thank you for beach boys, beach girls,
beach children, and beach music;
for fishermen and fisherwomen
and sand between your toes;
for wonderful places to visit and stay;
for good food and good company.

We thank you, too,
*   for worship ... for light.*
*   And the stars.*

*We are truly thankful
that there is no place
anywhere on Earth quite like this:
our state, our North Carolina.*

*May the Lord bless us and keep us
— just the way we are.*

PHOTO CREDITS
(in order of appearance)